ANDREW LLOYD WEBBER'S
NEW STAGE PRODUCTION
THE WIZARD OF OZ

CW00666147

Produced by
Alfred Music Publishing Co., Inc.
P.O. Box 10003
Van Nuys, CA 91410-0003
alfred.com

Printed in USA.

ISBN-10: 0-7390-8297-3
ISBN-13: 978-0-7390-8297-3

Photographs by Keith Pattison & Simon Turtle

Logo design by Dewynters
www.wizardofozthemusical.com

Nobody understands me   Nobody

...n listens

Nobody wants to help me

We're not in Kansas anymore

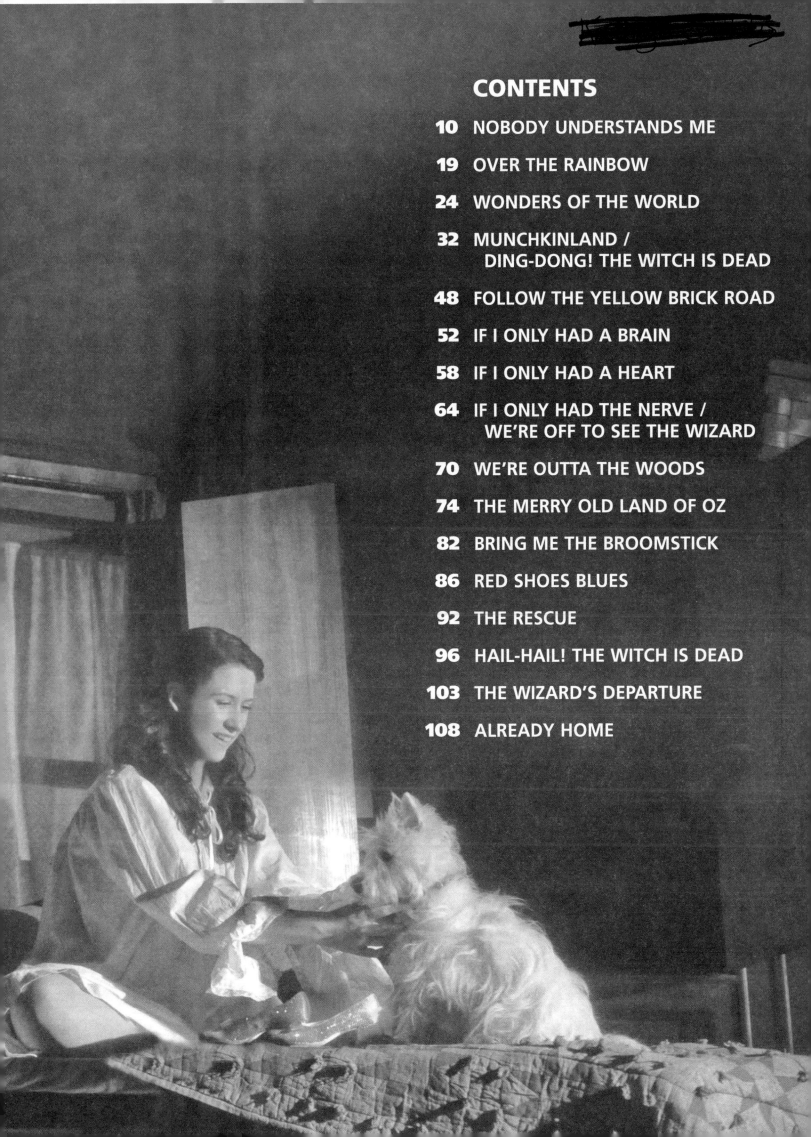

CONTENTS

NOBODY UNDERSTANDS ME

Lyrics by
TIM RICE

Music by
ANDREW LLOYD WEBBER

Moderately bright ♩. = 136

Dorothy:
No - bod - y un - der-stands me.

No - bod - y e - ven lis - tens.   No - bod - y wants to help me.

Nobody Understands Me - 9 - 1

12

Zeke:

When we were watering the crops.

Hunk:

Turn the hose on Miss Gulch?

Hickory:

Yeah, shall we do it again?

Zeke:

"I'll get you, and that girl, and her little dog too!"

Dorothy:

It's not funny. You play any more tricks,
you'll only make it worse.

Zeke, Hickory, Hunk:

Zeke:

Re - lax, she's not gon - na take_ him.

Dorothy:

But she will!

Hunk:

Dorothy:

But she means it!

Hunk/
Hickory:

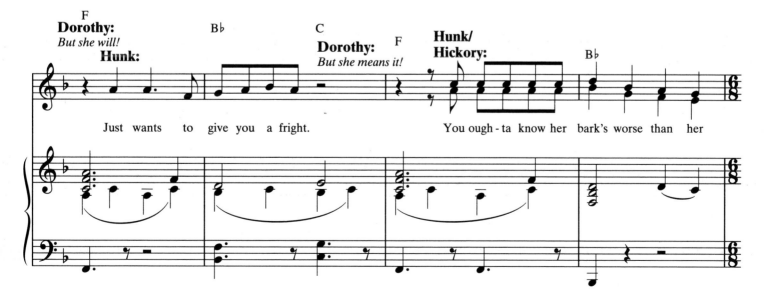

Just wants to give you a fright. You ough - ta know her bark's worse than her

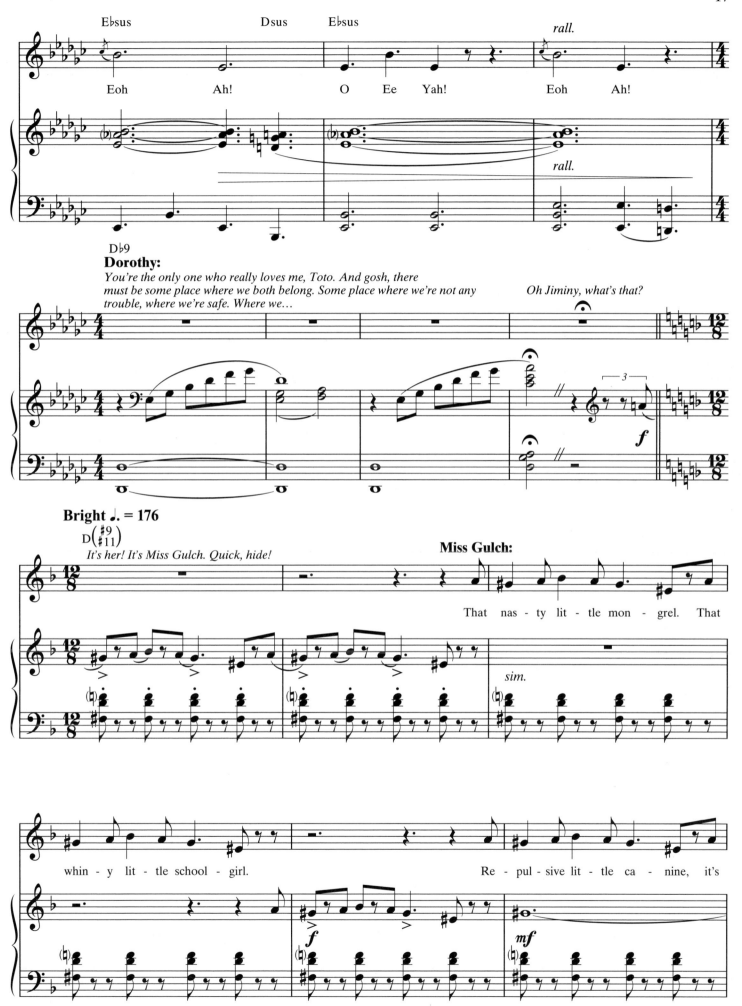

Segue to "Over the Rainbow"

OVER THE RAINBOW

Lyrics by
E.Y. HARBURG

Music by
HAROLD ARLEN

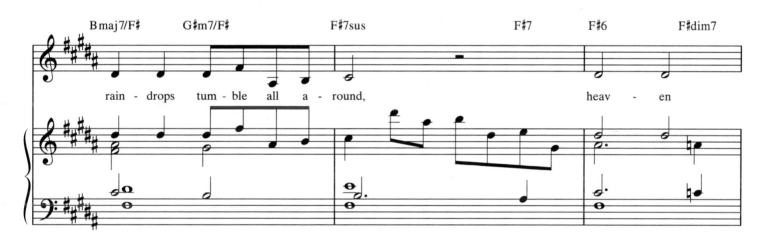

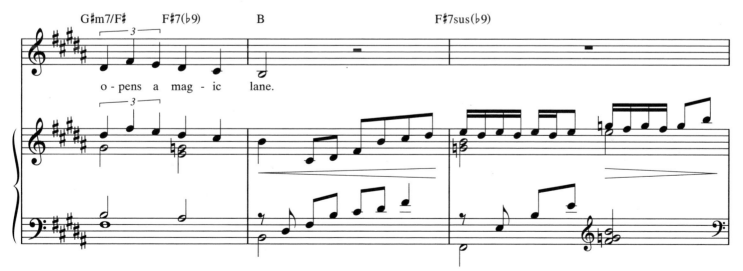

Over the Rainbow - 5 - 1

23

WONDERS OF THE WORLD

Lyrics by
TIM RICE

Music by
ANDREW LLOYD WEBBER

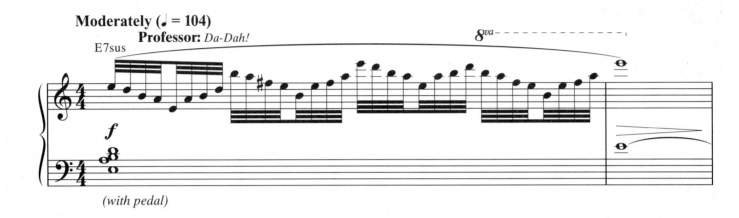

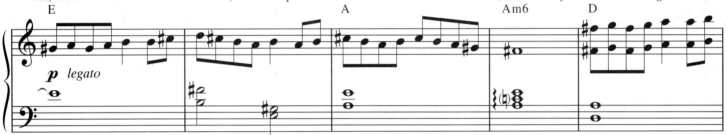

26

There's the Nile, now some don't give a hoot that it's the lon-gest riv-er, but we know in miles, of course, it's four-one-eight-y, sea to source, it's na-ture at its most pro-lif-ic, pyr-a-mids are quite ter-rif-ic too._____ So wel-come to the wait-ing won-ders of the world.

Some-times we may feel some-thing sim-ply can't be real, like a

road be - neath your feet that's paved with gold. I would be in-clined to main-

tain an o - pen mind, for truth is ver - y strange if truth be told.

più mosso

Here's old Po - po - ca - té - pe - tl, New York Cit - y glass and met - al, Ev - er - est un - con-quered moun-tain

o - ver five miles high and count-in'. Here the Arc-tic snows and po-lar bears and north-ern lights and so - lar

Professor & Dorothy:

home,_____ and home is one of man-y won-ders of the world. The

un-a-bridged as-sem-bled won-ders of the world. Pro-fes-sor Mar-vel's pat-ent won-ders

of the world._____

MUNCHKINLAND/DING-DONG! THE WITCH IS DEAD

Lyrics by
E.Y. HARBURG

Music by
HAROLD ARLEN

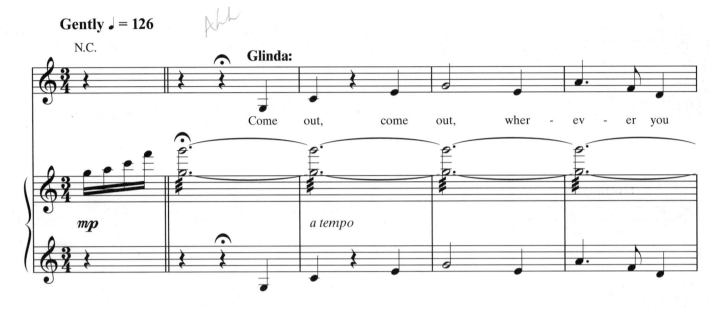

Glinda: Come out, come out, wher - ev - er you

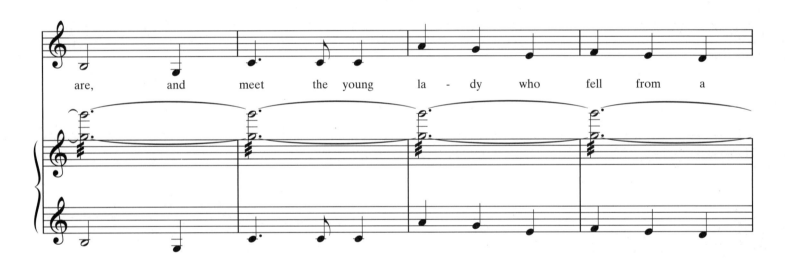

are, and meet the young la - dy who fell from a

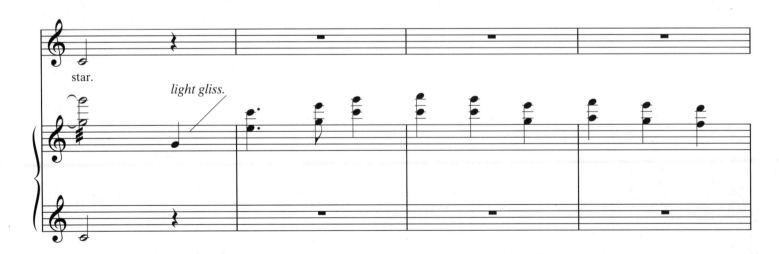

star.

light gliss.

Munchkinland/Ding-Dong! The Witch Is Dead - 16 - 1

34

36

FOLLOW THE YELLOW BRICK ROAD

Lyrics by
E.Y. HARBURG

Music by
HAROLD ARLEN

Slowly, freely (♩. = 80)

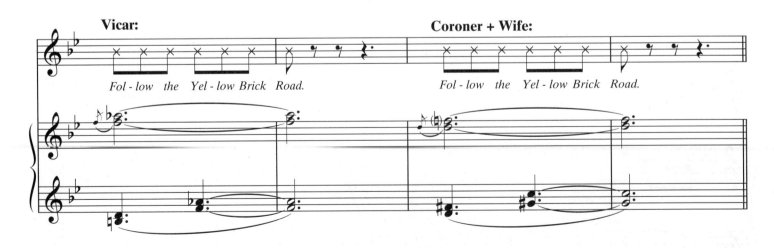

Follow the Yellow Brick Road - 4 - 1

IF I ONLY HAD A BRAIN

Lyrics by
E.Y. HARBURG

Music by
HAROLD ARLEN

If I Only Had a Brain - 5 - 2

54

IF I ONLY HAD A HEART

Lyrics by
E.Y. HARBURG

Music by
HAROLD ARLEN

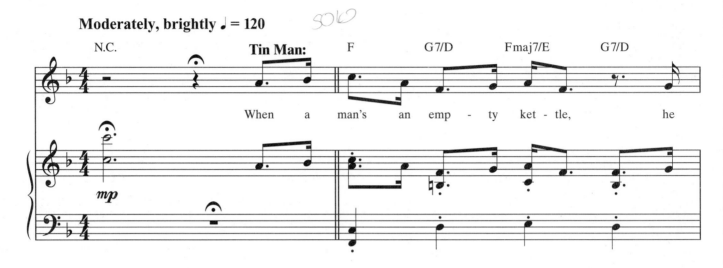

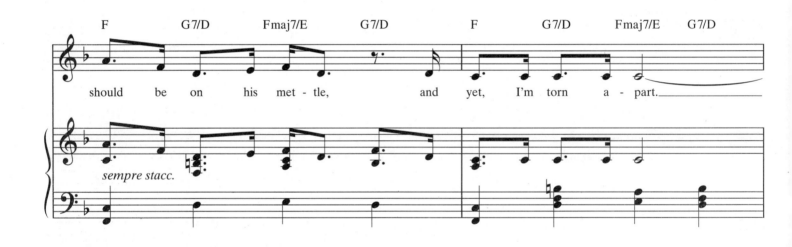

If I Only Had a Heart - 6 - 1

on - ly had a heart.

Just to

If I Only Had a Heart - 6 - 6

IF I ONLY HAD THE NERVE/
WE'RE OFF TO SEE THE WIZARD

Lyrics by
E.Y. HARBURG

Music by
HAROLD ARLEN

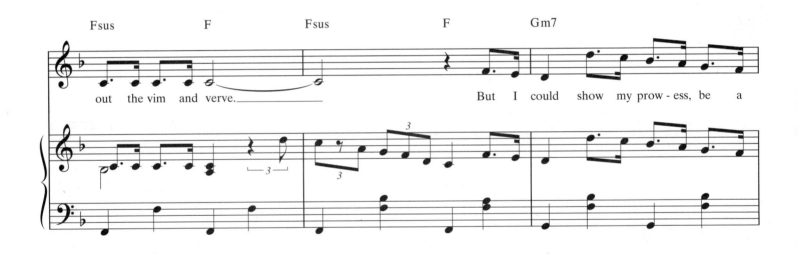

If I Only Had the Nerve/We're Off to See the Wizard - 6 - 1

WE'RE OUTTA THE WOODS

Lyrics by
E.Y. HARBURG

Music by
HAROLD ARLEN and
HERBERT STOTHART

Dorothy: *Look everybody; there, there in the distance. It's the Emerald City, and the Wizard,*

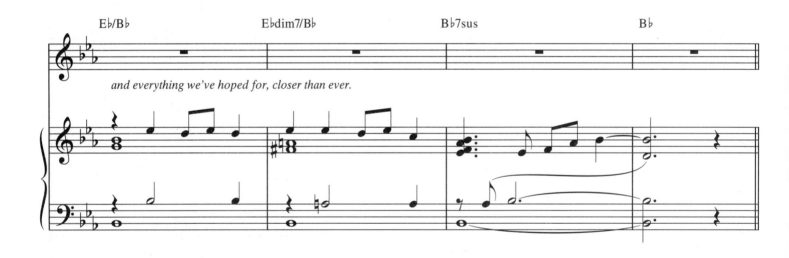

and everything we've hoped for, closer than ever.

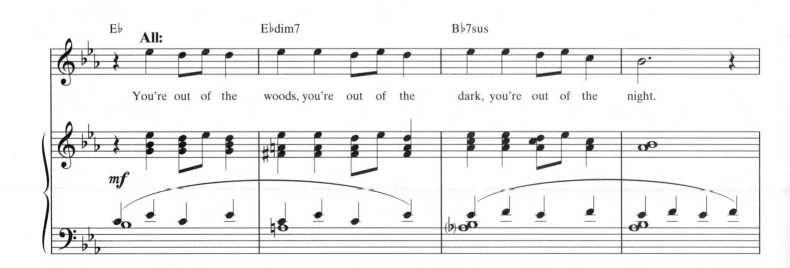

You're out of the woods, you're out of the dark, you're out of the night.

We're Outta the Woods - 4 - 1

72

We're Outta the Woods - 4 - 3

Hold on - to your breath, hold on - to your heart, hold on - to your

hope.

March up to that gate and bid it

o - pen,

o - pen,

o - pen.

Segue to "The Merry Old Land of Oz"

THE MERRY OLD LAND OF OZ

Lyrics by
E.Y. HARBURG

Music by
HAROLD ARLEN

76

The Merry Old Land of Oz - 8 - 3

The Merry Old Land of Oz - 8 - 4

BRING ME THE BROOMSTICK

Lyrics by
TIM RICE

Music by
ANDREW LLOYD WEBBER

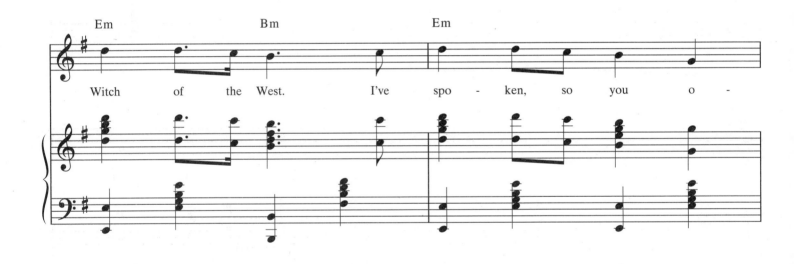

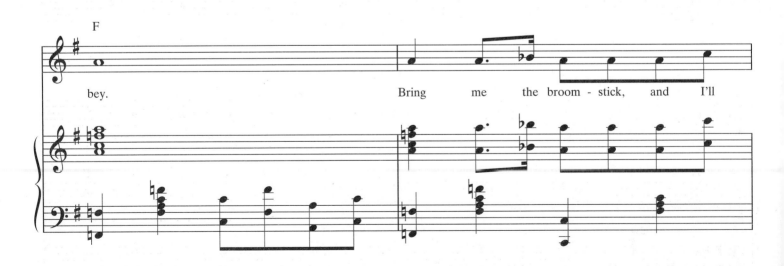

Witch of the West. These are your or-ders, now o - bey!

Presto ♩. = 160

RED SHOES BLUES

Lyrics by
TIM RICE

Music by
ANDREW LLOYD WEBBER

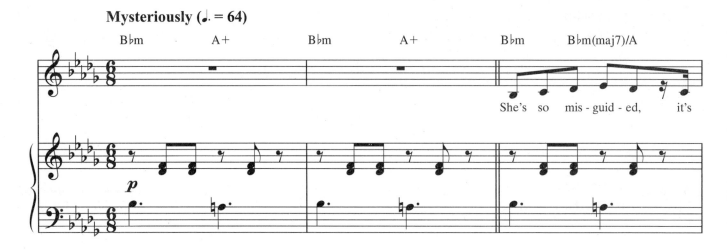

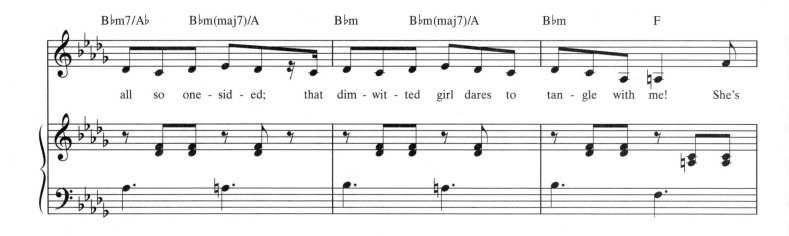

Red Shoes Blues - 6 - 1

88

Red Shoes Blues - 6 - 3

90

THE RESCUE

Music by
ANDREW LLOYD WEBBER

94

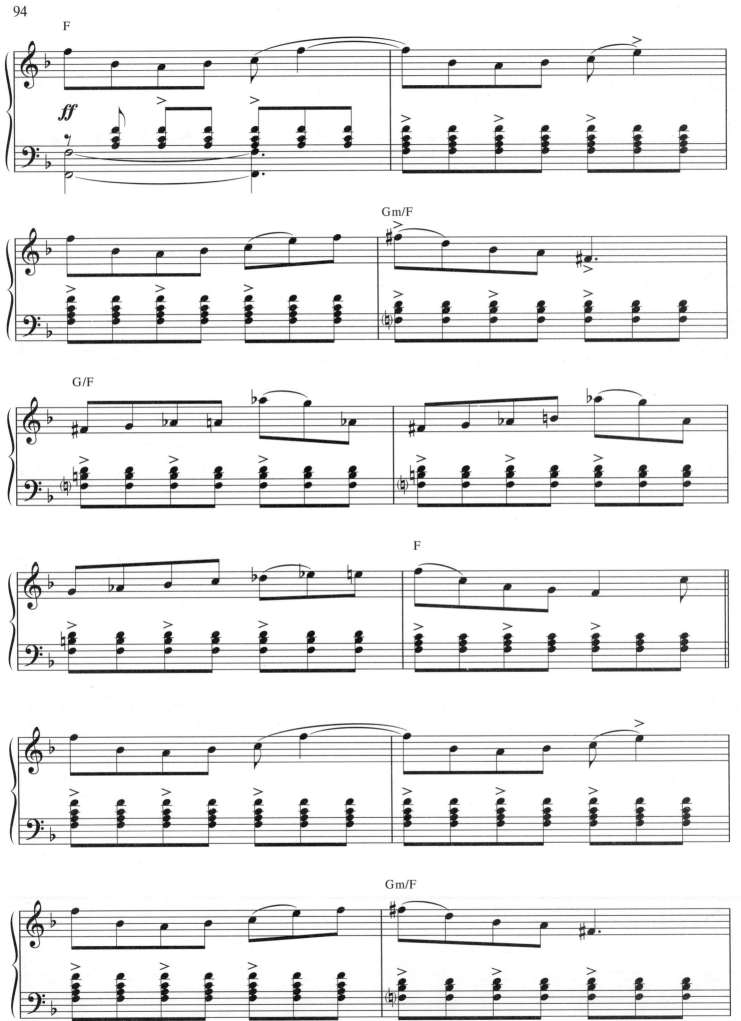

G/F

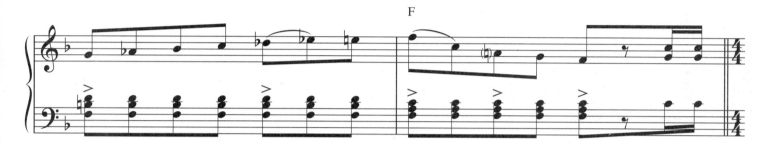

Moderate march ♩ = 128

F   C7   F   C7   F   F7(♭9)

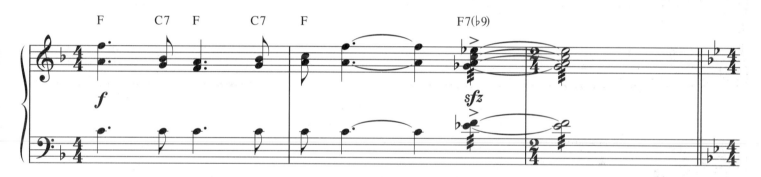

Slightly slower ♩ = 108

The Wicked Witch: *You cursed little brat! Look what you've done! I'm, I'm melting! Melting! Oh, what a world!*

N.C.

What a world! And to think a good little girl like you could destroy my beautiful wickedness! Help me! I'm melting! Melting!

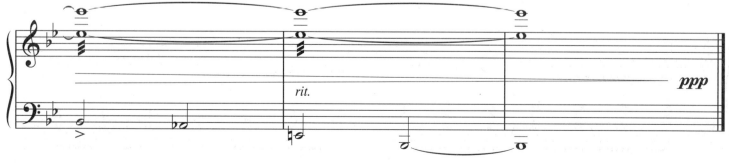

Seque to "Hail - Hail! The Witch Is Dead"

HAIL-HAIL! THE WITCH IS DEAD

Lyrics by
E.Y. HARBURG

Music by
HAROLD ARLEN

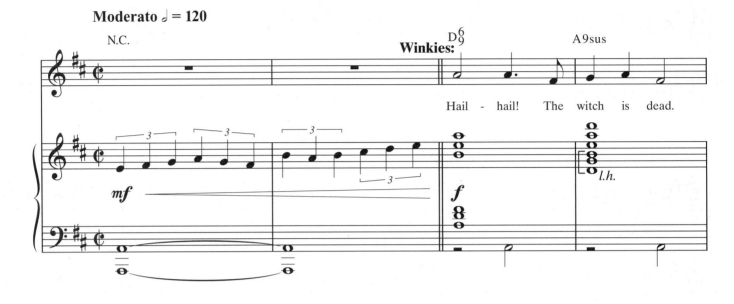

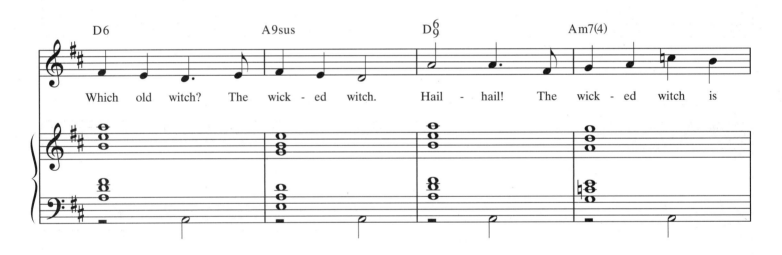

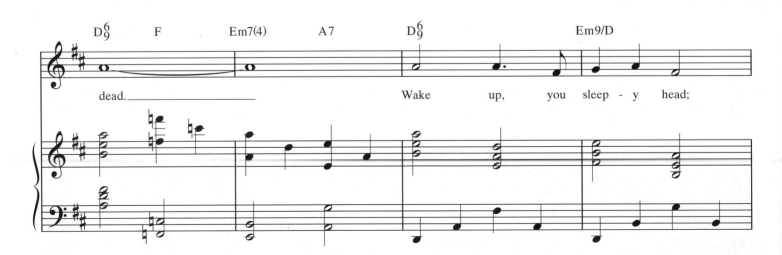

Hail-Hail! The Witch Is Dead - 7 - 1

THE WIZARD'S DEPARTURE

Lyrics by
TIM RICE

Music by
ANDREW LLOYD WEBBER

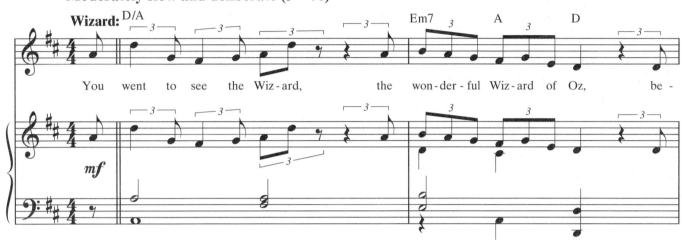

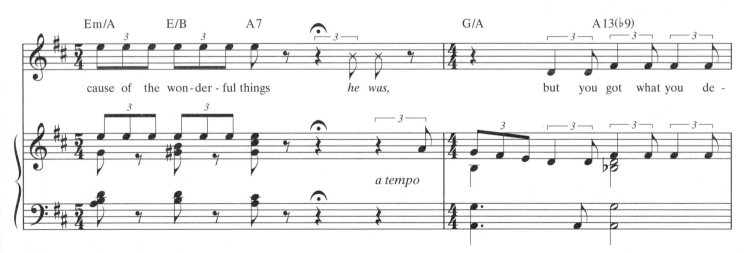

The Wizard's Departure - 5 - 1

serve: a brain,   a heart,   the nerve.

Slightly faster, flowing ♩ = 92

(with pedal)

The Wizard's Departure - 5 - 3

Dor-o-thy and I say a bit-ter-sweet good-bye, it's my plea-sure to hand o-ver to a

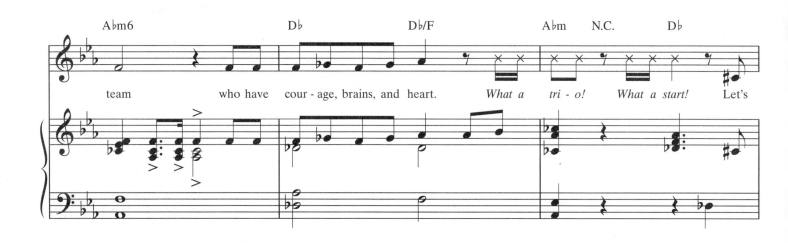

team who have cour-age, brains, and heart. *What a tri-o! What a start!* Let's

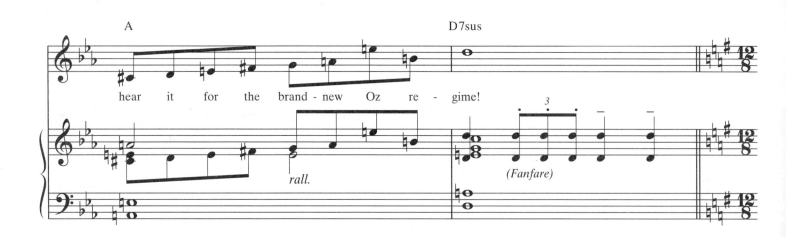

hear it for the brand-new Oz re-gime!

(Fanfare)

rall.

Allegro ♩. = 112

G

Wizard: *That's it! And obey them as you would me! And that's it!*

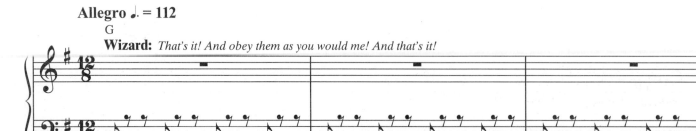

Dorothy: *Oh! Oh! Toto! He's seen a cat. Toto! Toto! It's only a cat! Oh! Oh! Don't go away!*

Toto! Come back!

Ab

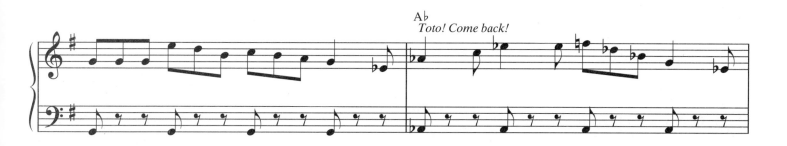

Wizard: *No! Off we go! No! No! Hold on to those lines!*

A

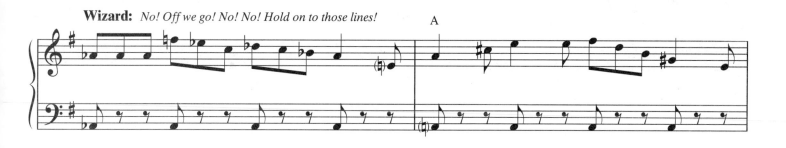

C#/A   D/A

That cat ruined my exit!

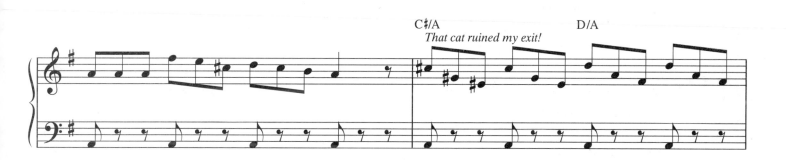

G/A   Ab/A   Bb   B

Dorothy: *Come back!*   **Wizard:** *Goodbye, folks!*

E/A   F/A

ALREADY HOME

Lyrics by
TIM RICE

Music by
ANDREW LLOYD WEBBER

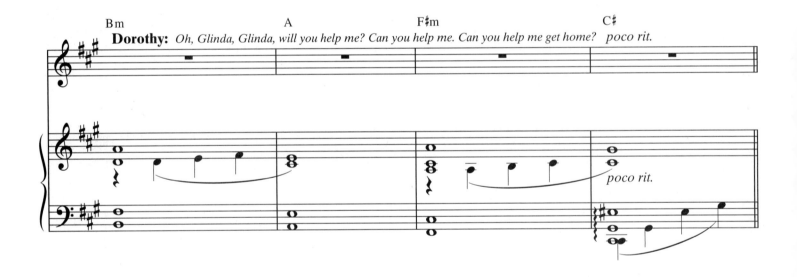

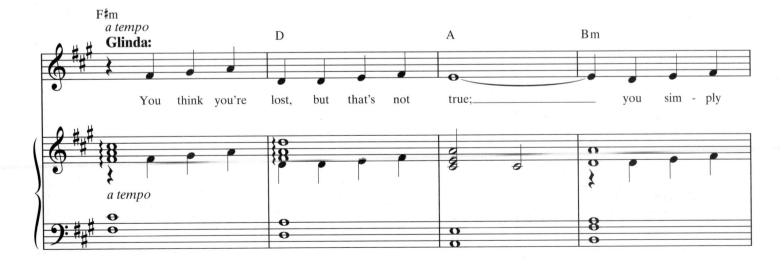

Already Home - 7 - 1

Ev - 'ry jour - ney leads you back to where you start.

Close your eyes, it's ver - y eas - y. You'll find that you're al - read - y

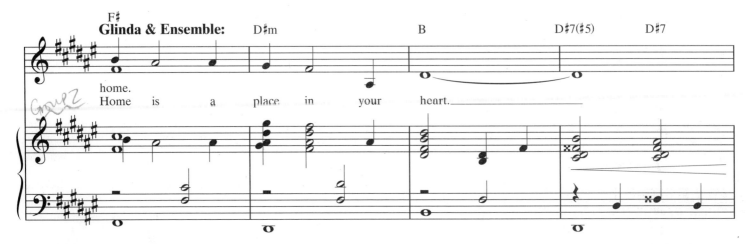

home.
Home is a place in your heart.

114

Already Home - 7 - 7

BELL OUT OF ORDER PLEASE KNOCK

Ding Dong The Witch is Dead

There's no place like...

Bill Kenwright and The Really Useful Group
present

Andrew Lloyd Webber's new production of

THE WIZARD OF OZ

with
MICHAEL CRAWFORD
as The Wizard

and
DANIELLE HOPE
as Dorothy

Music
HAROLD ARLEN

Lyrics
E.Y. HARBURG

Additional Lyrics
TIM RICE

Additional Music
ANDREW LLOYD WEBBER

Adapted by
ANDREW LLOYD WEBBER and **JEREMY SAMS**

Orchestrations
DAVID CULLEN

Musical Director
GRAHAM HURMAN

Projection Designer
JON DRISCOLL

Lighting Designer
HUGH VANSTONE

Sound Designer
MICK POTTER

Choreographer
ARLENE PHILLIPS

Set and Costume Designer
ROBERT JONES

Director
JEREMY SAMS

From the Book by L. Frank Baum
Based upon the Classic Motion Picture owned by Turner Entertainment
and produced with the permission of Warner Bros. Theatre Ventures and EMI Music Publishing